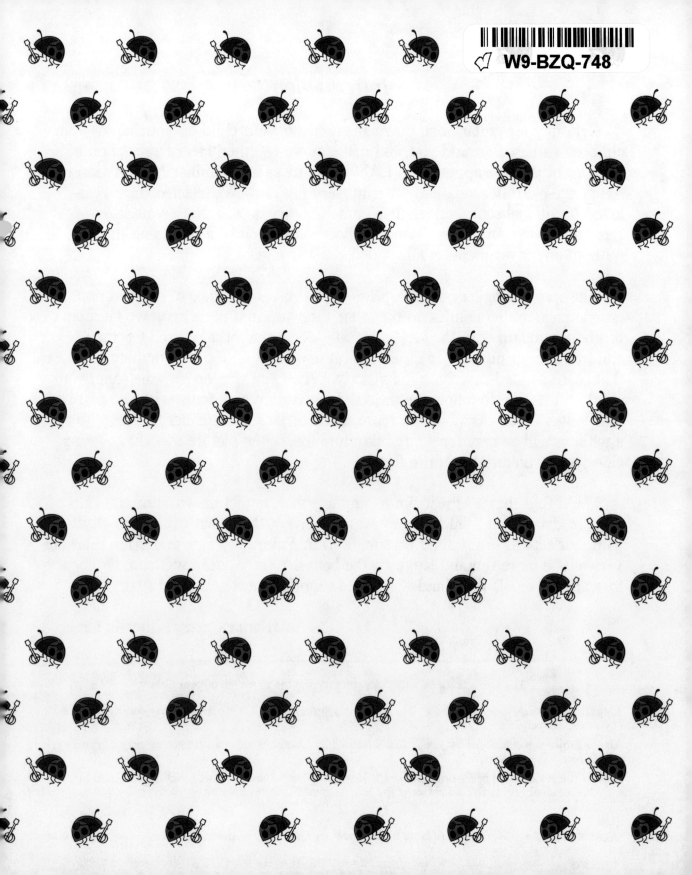

W9-BZQ-748

Introduction

Get out your guitar or sit down at the piano, your child on your lap or your children gathered around you, and make music together! Here's a selection of the songs that have appeared in LADYBUG magazine: familiar Mother Goose songs, age-old folk songs, and other nursery favorites. We selected these best-loved traditional songs, rather than contemporary ones, because you may remember them from your own childhood and you'll be able to sing them without any instruments at all.

The special magic of our songs lies in the correspondence of musical notes on one page to the pictures on the other. One hundred years ago, two German brothers came up with the idea of writing down the most beloved German children's songs not only in clear musical notation but also in little picture notes that corresponded exactly to the melody. When you sing or play the song, your child will be able to follow the melody by going up and down with the pictures. The longer or shorter notes are represented by larger or smaller figures. After a while it will be easy for your children to follow the picture melody and sing along with you and the entire family.

You'll find that it's great fun to sing together, to feel the rhythm and clap, rock, or dance to it. Children may want to invent their own words and rhythm games or actions or use their imaginations in making up new and often hilarious verses. The more fun and laughter, the better. Your children will come to look forward to "music time" and will ask to sing the songs again and again.

Marianne Carus, Editor-in-Chief

Here are a few easy songbooks you may want to check out of your library.

Songs from Mother Goose, compiled by Nancy Larrick, illustrated by Robin Spowart. Fifty-six rhymes with music. Harper, 1989.

The Lullaby Songbook, edited by Jane Yolen, illustrated by Charles Mikolaycak. Fifteen cherished lullabies. Harcourt Brace Jovanovich, 1986.

Singing Bee! A Collection of Favorite Children's Songs, compiled by Jane Hart, with pictures by Anita Lobel. One hundred twenty-five simple songs and singing games. Lothrop, Lee and Shepard, 1982.

SING TOGETHER WITH Ladybug®

Are You Sleeping?

Art by Becky Kelly

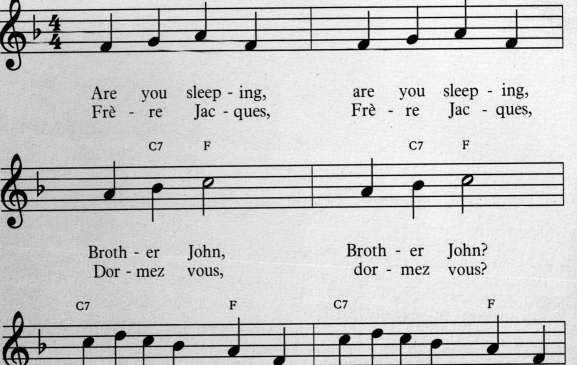

Are you sleep - ing,   are you sleep - ing,
Frè - re Jac - ques,   Frè - re Jac - ques,

Broth - er John,   Broth - er John?
Dor - mez vous,   dor - mez vous?

Morn - ing bells are ring - ing,   morn - ing bells are ring - ing,
Son - nez les ma - ti - nes,   son - nez les ma - ti - nes,

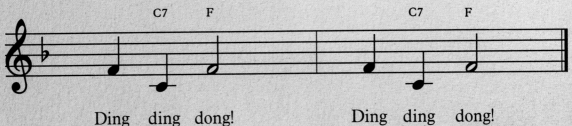

Ding ding dong!   Ding ding dong!
Din dan don!   Din dan don!

Are you sleep - ing, are you sleep - ing,
Frè - re Jac - ques, Frè - re Jac - ques,

Broth - er John, Broth - er John?
Dor - mez vous, dor - mez vous?

Morn - ing bells are ring - ing, morn - ing bells are ring - ing,
Son - nez les ma - ti - nes, son - nez les ma - ti - nes,

Ding ding dong! Ding ding dong!
Din din dan don! Din dan don!

5

ALPHABET SONG

Art by True Kelley

A, B, C, D, E, F, G, H, I, J, K, L, M, N, O, P

Q, R, S, and T, U, V, W,___ X, and Y, and Z.

Now I know my A B C s, Next time won't you sing with me?

A, B, C, D, E, F, G, H, I, J, K, L, M, N, O, P,

Q, R, S, and T, U, V, W,_____ X, and Y, and Z.

Now I know my A B Cs, Next time won't you sing with me?

Row, Row, Row Your Boat

Art by John Segal

Row, row, row your boat

Gent - ly down the stream.

Mer - ri - ly, mer - ri - ly, mer - ri - ly, mer - ri - ly,

Life is but a dream.

Row,   row,   row   your   boat

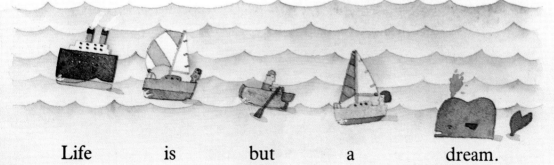

Gent   -   ly   down   the   stream.

Mer - ri - ly, mer - ri - ly, mer - ri - ly, mer - ri - ly,

Life   is   but   a   dream.

Hickory, Dickory, Dock

Art by Nadine Bernard Westcott

Hick - o - ry dick - o - ry dock,_____ the

mouse ran up the clock,_____ the clock struck one, the

mouse ran down, hick - o - ry dick - o - ry, dock._____

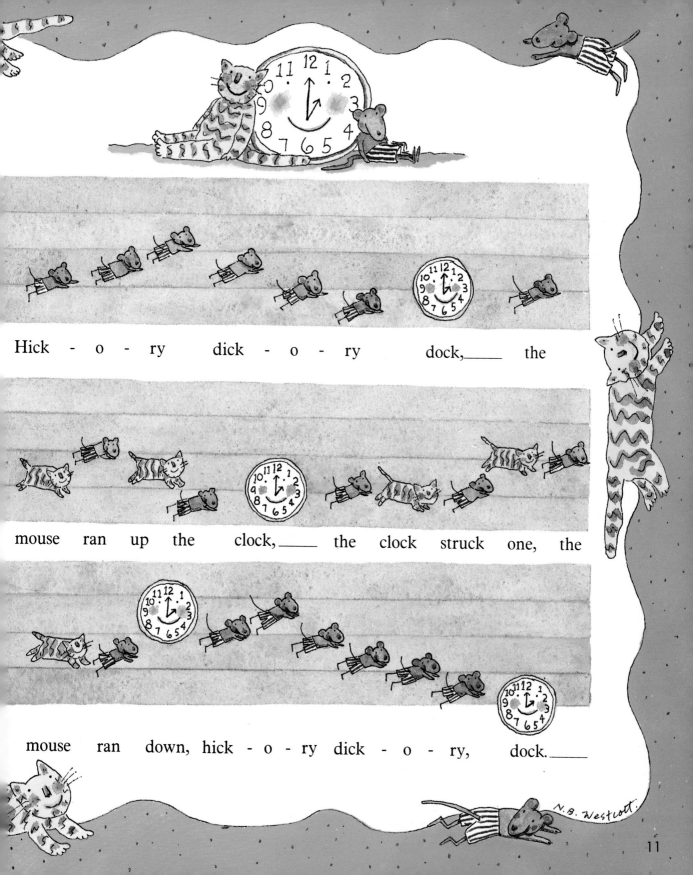

Hick - o - ry dick - o - ry dock,_____ the

mouse ran up the clock,_____ the clock struck one, the

mouse ran down, hick - o - ry dick - o - ry, dock._____

Mary Had a Little Lamb

Art by Becky Kelly

Ma - ry   had   a   lit - tle   lamb,

lit - tle   lamb,   lit - tle   lamb,

Ma - ry   had   a   lit - tle   lamb, its

fleece   was   white   as   snow.

Ma - ry   had   a   lit - tle   lamb,

lit - tle   lamb,   lit - tle   lamb,

Ma - ry   had   a   lit - tle   lamb, its

fleece   was   white   as   snow.

Skip to My Lou

Art by
Roni Shepherd

Lou, Lou, skip to my Lou;   Lou, Lou, skip to my Lou;

Lou, Lou, skip to my Lou;   Skip to my Lou, my   dar - ling.

Lit-tle red wag-on, paint-ed blue;   Lit-tle red wag-on, paint-ed blue;

Lit-tle red wag-on, paint-ed blue; Skip to my Lou, my dar - ling.

Lou, Lou, skip to my Lou; Lou, Lou, skip to my Lou;

Lou, Lou, skip to my Lou; Skip to my Lou, my dar - ling.

Lit-tle red wag - on, paint-ed blue; Lit-tle red wag-on, paint-ed blue;

Lit-tle red wag-on, paint-ed blue; Skip to my Lou, my dar - ling.

15

Ha! Ha! This-a-way

Art by Bonnie MacKain

Ha! ha! this‑a‑way, Ha! ha! that‑a‑way,

Ha! ha! this‑a‑way, Then oh then:

When I was a lit‑tle girl, lit‑tle girl, lit‑tle girl,
boy, boy, boy,

When I was a lit‑tle girl, five years old.
boy,

Ha! ha! this-a-way, Ha! ha! that-a-way,
Ha! ha! this-a-way, Then oh then:
I could stretch my arms up, arms up, arms up,
I could stretch my arms up, then oh then.

I could touch my shoulders,
shoulders, shoulders . . .

I could grab my ankles,
ankles, ankles . . .

I could snap my fingers,
fingers, fingers . . .

I could turn in circles,
circles, circles . . .

I could stand on one leg,
one leg, one leg . . .

I could hop in one place,
one place, one place . . .

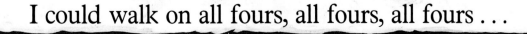

I could walk on all fours, all fours, all fours . . .

The Farmer in the Dell

Art by John Segal

The farm-er in the dell,

The farm-er in the dell,

Heigh - ho, the der - ry - o,

The farm-er in the dell.

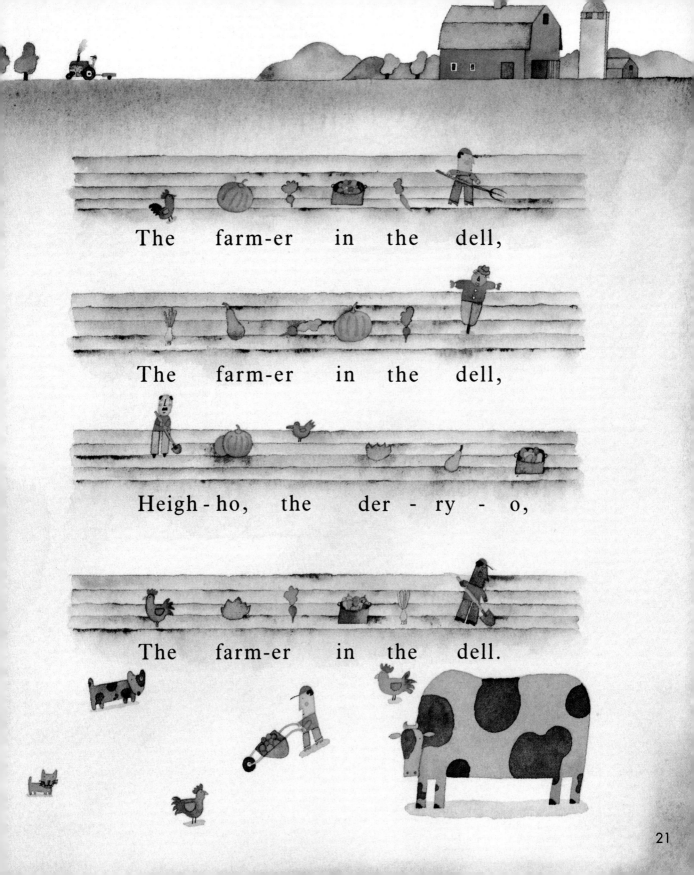

The farm-er in the dell,

The farm-er in the dell,

Heigh-ho, the der-ry-o,

The farm-er in the dell.

YANKEE DOODLE

Art by Nadine Bernard Westcott

Yan-kee Doo-dle went to town a - rid-ing on a po - ny,

Stuck a fea - ther in his hat and called it mac - a - ro - ni.

Yan-kee Doo-dle, keep it up! Yan-kee Doo-dle dan - dy,

Mind the mu-sic and the step, and with the girls be han - dy.

an - kee Doo - dle went to town a - rid - ing on a po - ny,

uck a fea - ther in his hat and called it mac - a - ro - ni.

Yan - kee Doo - dle, keep it up! Yan - kee Doo - dle dan - dy,

Mind the mu - sic and the step, and with the girls be han - dy.

23

Pop! Goes the Weasel

Art by Patience Brewster

All a-round the cob-bler's bench, the mon-key chased the wea-sel,

The mon-key thought 'twas all in fun.   Pop!   goes   the   wea-sel.

A pen-ny for a   spool of thread, a   pen-ny   for a   nee-dle,

That's the way the   mon-ey goes,   Pop!   goes   the   wea-sel.

All a - round the cob - bler's bench, the mon - key chased the wea - sel,

The mon - key thought 'twas all in fun. Pop! goes the wea - sel.

A pen - ny for a spool of thread, a pen - ny for a nee - dle,

That's the way the mon - ey goes, Pop! goes the wea - sel.

Looby Loo

Here we go loo-by loo, Here we go loo-by light,

Here we go loo-by loo, All on a Sat-ur-day night.

I put my right hand in, I put my right hand out,

I give my right hand a shake, shake, shake, And turn my-self a-bout.

Here we go loo - by loo, Here we go loo - by light,

Here we go loo - by loo, All on a Sat - ur - day night.

I put my right hand in, I put my right hand out,

I give my right hand a shake, shake, shake, And turn my-self a - bout.

Nadine B. Westcott.

Here we go looby loo,
Here we go looby light,
Here we go looby loo,
All on a Saturday night.

I put my left hand in,
I put my left hand out,
I give my left hand a shake, shake, shake,
And turn myself about.

Here we go looby loo,
Here we go looby light,
Here we go looby loo,
All on a Saturday night.

I put my right foot in,
I put my right foot out,
I give my right foot a shake, shake, shake,
And turn myself about.

Here we go looby loo,
Here we go looby light,
Here we go looby loo,
All on a Saturday night.

I put my left foot in,
I put my left foot out,
I give my left foot a shake, shake, shake,
And turn myself about.

Here we go looby loo,
Here we go looby light,
Here we go looby loo,
All on a Saturday night.

I put my whole self in,
I put my whole self out,
I give my whole self a shake, shake, shake,
And turn myself about.

Art by
Nadine Bernard Westcott

Twinkle, Twinkle, Little Star

Twin-kle, twin-kle, lit-tle star,   How I won-der what you are.

Up a-bove the   world so high, Like a dia-mond   in the sky,

Twin-kle, twin-kle, lit-tle   star,   How I won-der what you are.

Art by Kevin Hawkes

Twin-kle, twin-kle, lit-tle star,   How I won-der what you are.

FOLLOW THE STARS
AND THE OWLS' EYES!

Up a-bove the world so   high, Like a dia-mond   in the   sky,

Twin-kle, twin-kle, lit-tle   star,   How I won-der what you are.

Ten in the Bed

There were ten in the bed, and the lit - tle one said,

"Roll o - ver, roll o - ver."

So they all rolled o - ver and one fell out.

There were ten in the bed, and the lit - tle one said,

"Roll o - ver, roll o - ver."

So they all rolled o-ver and one fell out.

There were ten in the bed . . .

There were nine in the bed . . .

There were eight in the bed . . .

There were seven in the bed . . .

There were six in the bed . . .

There were five in the bed . . .

There were four in the bed . . .

There were three in the bed . . .

There were two in the bed
And the little one said,
"Roll over, roll over."
So they all rolled over
And one fell out.

There was one in the bed
And the little one said,
(*spoken*) "Good night!"

Art by Becky Kelly

Published by Carus Publishing Company
a division of Carus Corporation
Copyright © 1992 by Carus Publishing Company
All rights reserved. Printed in the U.S.A.

ISBN 0-8126-0079-7

Cover illustration by Bonnie MacKain

Grateful acknowledgment is made to the following copyright owners for permission to
reprint their material.
Patience Brewster for "Pop! Goes the Weasel," artwork © 1992 by Patience Brewster.
Kevin Hawkes for "Twinkle, Twinkle, Little Star," artwork © 1990 by Kevin Hawkes.
Becky Kelly for "Ten in the Bed," artwork © 1991 by Rebecca Kelly; "Mary Had a Little Lamb,"
artwork © 1991 by Rebecca Kelly; and "Are You Sleeping?" artwork © 1992 by Rebecca Kelly.
True Kelley for "Alphabet Song," artwork © 1991 by True Kelley.

Bonnie MacKain for "Ha! Ha! This-a-way," artwork © 1992 by Bonnie MacKain.
John Segal for "The Farmer in the Dell," artwork © 1990 by John Segal; and "Row, Row, Row
Your Boat," artwork © 1991 by John Segal.
Roni Shepherd for "Skip to My Lou," artwork © 1991 by Roni Shepherd.
Nadine Bernard Westcott, Inc. for "Looby Loo," artwork © 1991 by Nadine Bernard Westcott;
"Hickory, Dickory, Dock," artwork © 1991 by Nadine Bernard Westcott; and "Yankee Doodle,"
artwork © 1992 by Nadine Bernard Westcott.